Western Bark Beetle Strategy

Human Safety, Recovery and Resiliency
U. S. Forest Service

7/11/2011

The Western Bark Beetle Strategy identifies how the Forest Service is responding to and will respond to the western bark beetle epidemic over the next five years. The extent of the epidemic requires prioritization of treatments, first providing for human safety in areas threatened by standing dead hazard trees, and second, addressing dead and down trees that create hazardous fuels conditions adjacent to high value areas. After the priority of safety, forested areas with severe mortality will be reforested with the appropriate species (Recovery). Forests will also be thinned to reduce the number of trees per acre and create more diverse stand structures to minimize extensive epidemic bark beetle areas (resiliency). This is a modest strategy that reflects current budget realities, but focuses our resources in the most important places that we can make a big difference to the safety of the American public. This strategy covers Fiscal Year (FY) 2011 through 2016.

1

July 11, 2011

Table of Contents

Appendix 1 - Bark Beetle Funding and Projected Accomplishments for Fiscal Year 2011
Appendix 2 - Bark Beetle Projected Accomplishments (in acres) for Fiscal Years 2012-2016
Appendix 3 - Projected Capability (in acres) for Fiscal Years 2012 – 2016
Appendix 4 - Projected Research Funding for Fiscal Years 2011 – 2016
Appendix 5 – High Level Prioritization Model
Appendix 6 – Western Bark Beetle Initiative Success Stories

July 11, 2011

U.S. Forest Service

Western Bark Beetle Strategy for Human Safety, Recovery and Resiliency

Introduction:

The western United States is experiencing the largest bark beetle outbreak in recorded history.[1] Although western forests have experienced regular infestations throughout their history, the current epidemic is notable for its intensity, extensive geographic range, and simultaneous occurrence in multiple ecosystems. Since 1997, infestations of bark beetle species have escalated resulting in more than 41.7 million acres across all ownerships sustaining some level of conifer tree mortality (see Figure 1). The past decade's epidemic is unprecedented in its environmental and social impacts. Various parts of the west experienced bark beetle population peaks at different times over the past 14 years. For example from 2002-2005, Southern California experienced significant mortality from bark beetles[2]. The Forest Service and the Natural Resources Conservation Service undertook a focused safety and recovery effort that was supported by approximately $138 million in agency and supplemental appropriations. From 2000 through 2009, the intermountain west experienced bark beetle caused mortality over an estimated 21.7 million acres across all ownerships, 17.7 million acres on national forests.[3] The situation is further complicated by the fact that more and more people live and recreate in areas affected by the epidemic.

This strategy incorporates our current understanding of available scientific research and presents a science-based path forward. The strategy will be achieved through well-defined goals, objectives, and action items, to address each of the three prongs of the bark beetle problem: human safety, forest recovery, and long-term forest resiliency. A successful approach to mitigating the impact of bark beetle must address actions for all three goals. While safety of human communities and infrastructure protection is paramount, there is also a critical need to restore the function and structure of our forests. Bark beetle is a natural part of our forests and as such will regularly impact our forests and the adjacent communities. Conducting resiliency treatments now and in the future will help minimize the potential for new outbreaks of bark beetles or make future outbreaks less intense.

Although there has been much work accomplished to date for bark beetle management, this report focuses on the future. Honing our continuing response will seek to integrate various vegetation management activities across all jurisdictions to address bark beetle concerns in prioritized areas. Specific activities will be funded under specific programs (Recreation, Road Management, Trail Management, Forest Health Protection, Hazardous Fuels, Facilities Maintenance, Forest Management, Vegetation Management and Salvage Sale Fund, and the Integrated Recovery and Restoration Fund if authorized in FY 2012) but the integration of these programs is necessary to achieve the maximum

---

[1] Bentz, et. al. (2009) Bark Beetle Outbreaks in Western North America: Causes and Consequences, Bark Beetle Symposium, Snowbird, Utah.

[2] USDA Forest Service (2006) Forest Insect and Disease Conditions in the United States 2005. USDA Forest Service.

[3] USDA Forest Service (2010) Major Forest Insect and Disease Conditions in the United States: 2009 Update. USDA Forest Service FS-952.

amount of work. However, the scale of the treatment needed even in the priority areas, would require the Agency to shift additional funding to accomplish all of the work proposed by this Strategy. Now is the time to act. Forest Service resources are in a position in which they can effectively respond and address this issue with increased effort. Public safety and economic impacts and costs will only increase if we delay.

Background:
Across the landscape from the West Coast through the Rocky Mountains, bark beetles have affected more than 41.7 million acres of conifer forests since 1997, 21.7 million acres in the intermountain west alone. Other specific "hot spots" are in southeastern Oregon and northeastern Washington. Damage from spruce beetle in Alaska occurred before 1997 and is not shown on the map (Figure 1). In 2009 alone, more than eight million acres were newly infested by mountain pine bark beetle and it is expected that this outbreak will continue to expand through the near future (5-10 years). The agency has consistently focused on bark beetle activity with regular program funding. This has been effective in most situations for responding to limited outbreaks that are more limited in scope. The current situation is beyond the scale where we have been able to effectively respond with regular program funding, so we must prioritize locations.

If pine forests have not been thinned to encourage vigorous trees that better fend off beetles, upon maturity they become predisposed to bark beetle attack. As these beetle populations build up they can create huge epidemics. This is the situation we face today. Across vast acres in the West, even-aged stands of pine forests have formed as a result of years of fire suppression and large-scale, intense logging at the turn of the century. Many of these tree species life histories are fire-adapted, and lodgepole pine, for example, naturally regenerates in the presence of fire. These homogeneous and overly dense forests have provided an extensive food source for beetles, and they have responded with large population build-ups. In addition, climate change has resulted in warmer winters that have not been cold enough to reduce beetle populations. This phenomenon, combined with multi-year drought, has allowed beetles to proliferate at higher elevations and latitudes and has resulted in more beetle generations per year in some areas. On average, yearly bark beetle-caused tree mortality is about equal to wildland fire tree mortality across the US.[4][5]

With more people recreating and living in and/or adjacent to forested areas, this epidemic has affected high public use areas causing significant human safety concerns. The U.S. Forest Service estimates that up to 100,000 dead trees killed by beetles fall to the ground every day in southern Wyoming and northern Colorado. Many standing, bark beetle-killed trees pose significant safety threats around roads, trails and facilities (such as buildings and campgrounds). In the Interior West alone, there are approximately 14,000 miles of roads, trails, and right-of-ways that could be adversely affected by falling trees, as well as approximately 1,400 recreation sites. Numerous power lines and municipal water supply reservoirs are also at risk from the dangers of falling dead trees. Health and safety activities are ongoing, but the need is growing as beetles move into new areas.

---

[4] Smith, W. Brad, et al. (2009) Forest Resources of the United States, 2007. A technical document supporting the Forest Service 2010 RPA Assessment. USDA Forest Service GTR-WO-78.
[5] USDA Forest Service (2010) Major Forest Insect and Disease Conditions in the United States: 2009 Update. USDA Forest Service FS-952

July 11, 2011

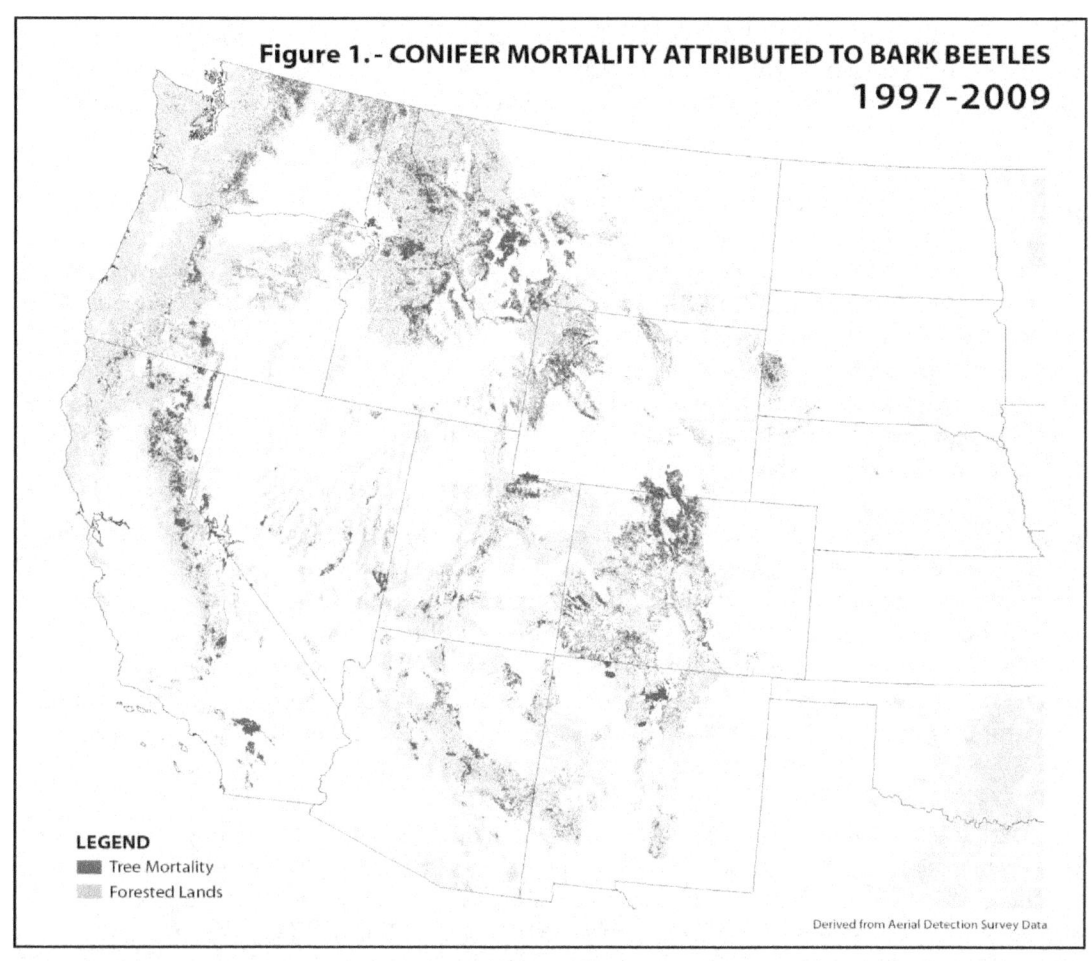

Figure 1.- CONIFER MORTALITY ATTRIBUTED TO BARK BEETLES 1997-2009

LEGEND
■ Tree Mortality
▨ Forested Lands

Derived from Aerial Detection Survey Data

ACRES BY STATE

Arizona	2,343,000
California	5,528,000
Colorado	6,637,000
Idaho	5,177,000
Montana	6,166,000
Nebraska	30,000
Nevada	1,302,000
New Mexico	1,830,000
Oregon	3,000,000
South Dakota	473,000
Utah	1,960,000
Washington	3,622,000
Wyoming	3,654,000
TOTAL ACRES	41,722,000

BARK BEETLES INCLUDED

California fivespined ips	Pine engraver
Douglas-fir beetle	Pinyon ips
Douglas-fir engraver	Red turpentine beetle
Douglas-fir pole beetle	Roundheaded pine beetle
Fir engraver	Silver fir beetle
Ips pilifrons	Southern pine beetle
Ips spp.	Spruce beetle
Jeffrey pine beetle	Western balsam bark beetle
Lodgepole pine beetle	Western cedar bark beetle
Mountain pine beetle	Western pine beetle
Phloeosinus spp.	

In addition to the danger of dead trees falling on people and infrastructure, beetle outbreaks create a fire hazard, which is especially relevant in the Wildland Urban Interface (WUI) and municipal watersheds. Due to the dead needles retained in the tree's crown, fire hazard increases one to two years after pine trees die.

These needles (red-needle phase) stock the canopy with dry, fine fuels that can ignite quickly during weather conditions conducive to fire.[6] Canopy fires are notably difficult to suppress. The overall risk posed by fire temporarily decreases after the dead needles have fallen while the trees remain standing (0 to 10 years after the trees are attacked). From 10-20 years onward, the fire hazard increases again. As dead branches and trees fall, a heavy fuel bed is created, which poses an increased risk of a surface fire.[7] The outbreak increases the number of acres of municipal watersheds and WUI in need of treatment to protect communities and infrastructure from fire. Additionally, due to the lack of safe egress and intense burning conditions created by standing beetle killed trees or down heavy slash, fighting these types of fires is extremely dangerous to fire fighters.

While the immediate safety concerns posed by hazard trees and fire (in the WUI) are critical, ecological recovery also must not be forgotten. Forests play a critical role in providing clean water, wildlife habitat, and a variety of recreation opportunities and rural jobs. The current infestation has increased fire hazard in some fire –prone areas near population centers and modified wildlife habitats. Tree mortality resulting from infestations have also impaired the ability of forests in high-elevation watersheds to provide shade and shelter that help to maintain the winter snow pack and prevent quick runoff during the spring melt and summer storms. In some areas, the existence of high-elevation, five-needle pine species are severely threatened by bark beetles, white pine blister rust, and climate change.[8]

Ecological resiliency of the affected forests needs to be addressed to reduce the frequency and scale of future epidemics. This is a long-term commitment that we have been working towards for years. Without significant changes in weather or forest structure, there is a potential for even more forested acres across the West to be infested by bark beetles. At the landscape scale, stands with low tree densities, and species and stand diversity can help reduce susceptibility to bark beetles. For example, healthy ponderosa pine forests need to be thinned over time by either wildfire or mechanical harvest to reduce density and, thereby decrease vulnerability to beetle attack. The health of lodgepole pine forests, whose stands are naturally dense, is improved when there is variety of stand ages positioned across a landscape.

Agency Approach: Priorities

It is clear the agency cannot treat every forest acre or mile of road that needs attention. Thus, the agency has developed a set of priorities to address safety, recovery and resilience to be as responsive as possible within the current budget environment. The projected level of funding for bark beetle management

---

[6] Page, W.; Jenkins, M. 2007. Mountain pine beetle-induced changes to selected lodgepole pine fuel complexes within the intermountain region. Forest Science 53(4):507-518.
[7] Bentz, et. al. (2009) Bark Beetle Outbreaks in Western North America: Causes and Consequences, Bark Beetle Symposium, Snowbird, Utah.
[8] Gibson, Ken, et al Mountain Pine Beetle Impacts in High-Elevation Five-Needle Pines: Current Trends and Challenges. R1-08-020, September 2008

demonstrates the agency's commitment to respond to the situation. However, current budget constraints require the Forest Service to respond to the highest priority needs.

Safety- When trees die in or adjacent to administrative areas, there is a potential for falling trees to injure or kill people. When trees die along roads and trails, there is a potential for falling trees to block ingress/egress hindering emergency operations. Due to bark beetles, this has become a major safety issue as a result of the number of falling dead trees. Trees have died in many different types of areas: some near people, some in remote areas. We will target dead trees in areas near people because where there is a significant possibility dead trees can injure people and property by falling, there must be mitigation. (See Figure 2.) Significance of hazard will be assessed using the hazard tree assessment rating system. Many roads and trails have been impacted creating an urgent safety issue that also must be addressed in a timely manner. Dead trees can fall and block egress during emergency evacuations. This is exacerbated by the high winds usually associated with wildfires. Main evacuation corridors will be identified in communities and a portion of the bark beetle funds will be used to prevent dead trees from blocking these routes during emergencies. The routes identified will be prioritized to determine the sequence in which they will be treated. In addition to hazard tree removal, temporary closure of areas, roads, trails, and sites, and fuel reduction treatments are actions that will be used to mitigate public safety hazards.

Prioritization of hazard tree removal work will be based upon regional prioritization of local risk assessments that evaluate potential exposure to people of the hazard associated with falling dead trees and increased fire risk due to fuel build up. In particular, hazard tree reduction will be focused on the high public use areas, such as campgrounds and parking areas. Fuel reduction work using hazardous fuels funds will be focused on treatments in the WUI, prioritized using local Community Wildfire Protection Plans. Municipal watersheds and high-use campgrounds will have fuel hazards mitigated through integrated projects using Hazardous Fuels or Integrated Resource Restoration funds (or equivalent). Roads and trails will be prioritized based on level of use, maintenance levels, egress/ingress for fire equipment, designation as corridors in community evacuation plans, and access for administrative sites. Treatments within the boundary of special use permits (for example, power lines, ski areas, etc.) will be prioritized and treatments will be accomplished through partnerships.

Figure 2. Examples of bark beetle mortality threatening a trail (right) and a power line (left) that would be a priority for human safety treatment. Region 2, Forest Service.

Recovery - As the safety work referenced above is completed, there is a less time-sensitive, but important task of rehabilitating areas to restore proper ecological functioning condition (Figure 3). As before, more land is in need of work than we can treat, so we will prioritize our work to focus in the most important places. Some of this recovery work will occur in areas that were treated for safety issues. Other recovery work will need to occur in areas that were not public safety concerns, but still need attention to restore functioning condition. As in the safety discussion, these recovery

Figure 3. Example of a campground ready for recovery treatments following removal of bark beetle killed trees. Region 2, Forest Service.

areas may or may not have been highlighted in the National Insect and Disease Risk Map (NIDRM) effort. Forest recovery will go hand in hand with other agency efforts including the Cohesive Fire Strategy, the Watershed Condition Framework and State Assessments and Strategies. Recovery will help us to restore a diverse and healthy working forest that supports an abundance and diversity of wildlife, provides clean water and contributes to local economies. Prioritization of recovery treatments will be based upon regional and local assessments that consider municipal watersheds, threatened and endangered species habitats, fire risk, and accessibility. Within the national Western Bark Beetle Strategy, each Region's approach and criteria will vary based upon regional priorities and the phase of bark beetle infestations. The spruce beetle epidemic in Alaska is over and some recovery work may take place in Alaska using regular agency program funds.

Management actions could include: the removal of dead trees, which have the potential to increase fuel loads; cone collections of blister rust resistant five-needle pine species; planting trees after fuel treatments to accelerate habitat restoration and the occupancy of the site by vegetation; and noxious weed treatments or seeding with native species to prevent noxious weed establishment. Recovery will factor effects of climate change.

Resilience – In addition to dealing with the consequences of bark beetle infestations, across the West, is given to consideration positioning western forests to be more resilient to approaching infestations. NIDRM specifically identifies these areas—areas that in the future are projected to experience nearly three times the level of normal mortality as a result of bark beetle activity. Resilience in this document connotes actions occurring to help ensure forests and grasslands can respond to disturbances that cause stress as quickly as possible, so that ecological functions and goods and services can still accrue from impacted lands. Resiliency is the ability of forests to survive stress – drought, insect attack, or disease – bark beetle prevention in one sense. Reducing the relative competition for moisture, nutrients, sunlight between trees reduces stress and enables trees to withstand stress causing situations, such as bark beetle attack.

Thinning forests to reduce the number of trees per acre and to create more diverse forest stand structure is the primary action to improve resiliency (Figure 4)[9]. Thinning treatments will be applied where they will have a positive impact. Spraying or injection of insecticides may be used to protect individual,

Figure 4. Before (left) and after (right) thinning of dense pine stands that were highly susceptible to bark beetle attacks and catastrophic wildfire. Region 5, Forest Service.

high value trees from bark beetle attack in certain rare situations (Figure 5). The relative priority of resiliency treatments compared to safety and recovery will be guided by the phase of epidemic occurring within a Region; between Regions; and between National Forest System lands and adjacent state, private and tribal forests.

Figure 5. High value tree being sprayed to protect against bark beetle attack is an example of a resiliency treatment. Region 3, Forest Service.

The peer-reviewed 2006 NIDRM, with an update to be released in 2011, serves as the backbone of forest health management for the Forest Service, and will play a large role in the **prioritization of resiliency efforts**. The risk map depicted in this report (see Figure 6) is a subset portraying just bark beetle insects. NIDRM indicates 20 million acres at risk to 25% mortality or more from western bark beetles over the 2006-2021 time period; there are 29 million acres at risk nationwide. However, many of these acres are in areas that are a lower priority for treatment, such as wilderness, roadless or inoperable areas. **This leaves approximately 9.0 million acres across all land ownerships available as the main focus for treatment.**

We know that of these 9.0 million acres in the West in need of treatment, there are about 525,000 acres at risk across all ownerships that are located in the WUI (which most greatly impact property values, public safety, and people's well being) and 1.87 million acres in impaired municipal watersheds, which we will consider to be the highest priority for treatments[10]. See Appendix 5 for a model

---

[9] Fettig, C.J., Klepzig, K.D., Billings, R.F., Munson, A. S., Nebeker, T.E., Negron, J.F. and Nowak, J.T. 2007. The effectiveness of vegetation management practices for prevention and control of bark beetle infestations in coniferous forests of the western and southern United States. Forest Ecology and Management 238:24-53.

[10] Forest Health Technology Enterprise Team. Personal communication.

9

displaying this relationship. Some, but not all of these priority acres overlap. Over the next five years, the agency intends to treat a significant percent of these high priority acres through thinning or annual insecticide applications. Forest Service Regions will work closely with their partners to customize their priorities to conduct preventative treatment that will protect the WUI, critical infrastructure, and municipal watersheds based upon existing programs of work.

In the southern US, almost 1 million acres of high priority acres have been treated to address their Southern Pine Beetle problem since 2002. They provide an excellent model to follow for this portion of the work to be accomplished as laid out in this report which restricted to the West.

Figure 6. National Insect and Disease Risk Map: Bark Beetle Risk.

Agency Approach: Performance

Tracking agency bark beetle efforts will be accomplished within existing performance measures. This includes effectiveness monitoring and tracking treatments spatially to evaluate that treatments are being implemented effectively. These measures will record outputs specifically tied to bark beetle efforts such as, road and trail hazard miles mitigated, recreation site hazards mitigated, and hazardous fuels acres treated. Regions will report beetle-related accomplishments using the pre-existing agency reporting system. Acres listed are estimates of performance expected and subject to change from a variety of factors.

July 11, 2011

Goals, Objectives and Actions:

It is clear that the bark beetle infestation presents a three-pronged problem. One, the current infestation creates a **human safety** problem from falling trees and subsequent increased wildfire hazard; two, ecosystem **recovery** is impaired in forests across the west and the increased fire hazard may further compromise ecosystem services such as clean water, clean air, and wildlife habitat; and three, without human intervention to alter forest conditions and increase the **resilience** of western forests, severe beetle outbreaks will continue and expand in the near-term.

A number of research needs are identified to support the three goals. Research recommended by this strategy may take more time from study design to having measureable results than the timeframe covered by this strategy. Current research results on bark beetles include lifecycle, control and suppression methods, and interactions with climate change. However, the new research to address of epidemic specific human safety, recovery and resilience science gaps identified by managers in the strategy, expands their existing science-based management options, are necessary to improve our ability to effectively manage forested landscapes susceptible to bark beetle epidemic, and results will be applicable beyond the strategy period.

The Forest Service will maintain the Fiscal Year 2010 level of funding ($101.5 million) in Fiscal Year 2011. This level of funding will be maintained for Fiscal Years 2012-2016, assuming appropriations in the out years at the 2010 level. The extent of potential bark beetle work identified will need additional time to fully accomplish the program of work identified in this strategy assuming flat funding.

Goal 1: Safety: Ensure that people and community infrastructure are protected from the hazards of falling bark beetle-killed trees and elevated wildfire potential.

The Forest Service's increased emphasis on safety compels us to do everything possible to aggressively mitigate and prevent falling trees from harming people and infrastructure. In the first two years of a bark beetle outbreak, when dead trees still have red needles, in the WUI there is an increased fire hazard that can be ameliorated through immediate fuel treatments. Coordination will occur with other State and federal agencies and partners to determine the risk to human safety, communicate the risks to the public, and leverage available partner capacity and funds to increase the scope of projects.

> Funding: FY 2011, $84.8 million
> Goal Performance[11] measure: FY 2011 – 187,800 Acres of treatment; FY 2012 – 240,026 Acres of treatment; FY 2013-2016 – 1,270,199 Acres of treatment.

Objective 1: Mitigate falling tree hazards to people and community infrastructure

> **Action Item A:** Remove hazard trees along the highest priority roads, trails, and recreation sites and facilities. **Performance measure:** miles of road/trail treated; number of sites treated.

---

[11] For all goal areas, FY-2011 is the actual planned accomplishment resulting from the planned funding from the President's Budget Request. The accomplishments planned for FY-2012-16 are based the maximum ability of the Forest Service. The actual accomplishment by Fiscal Year will depend on the actual funding available in each Fiscal Year.

Action Item B: Facilitate permittees completing hazard tree mitigation on lands under special use authorization (for example, power lines or ski areas). **Performance measure:** number of miles treated; numbers of sites treated; value of areas protected.

Action Item C: Develop and implement a mechanism to adequately warn the public of falling tree hazards in untreated areas or sites. This should effectively communicate to the public what the hazards are to effectively allow them to plan use of affected national forest areas or sites. In some cases specific roads and administrative sites may be closed. **Performance measure:** Hazard communication plan and actions implemented.

Action Item D: Synthesize and conduct research to describe site-specific factors that influence the fall rate of bark beetle-killed trees.
Performance measure: Number of research tools developed and applied to management on the ground.

Objective 2: Decrease fire hazard primarily related to elevated risk of crown fire immediately after beetle infestation.

Action Item A: Complete highest priority fuel treatments in municipal watersheds, the WUI, adjacent to community infrastructure, and around high-use recreation and administrative sites.
Performance measure: number of priority acres treated; value areas protected.

Action Item B: Synthesize and conduct research to improve the ability of fuel and fire behavior models to predict the influence of standing dead trees in bark beetle kill areas. Include research to determine how bark beetle outbreaks alter fuel complexes over time and apply fire behavior models to beetle-killed forests to evaluate fire behavior and fire risk related to age of mortality and to assess the effectiveness of fuel treatments and fire breaks established in the landscape.
Performance measure: Number of research tools developed and applied to management on the ground.

Objective 3: Encourage optimal utilization of material removed from beetle-killed forests, benefitting local communities through job creation and potentially decreasing the cost of forest treatments.

Action Item A: Develop strategies and infrastructure for removing standing dead trees from beetle-infested forests, including working with the private sector to develop small mills for solid wood processing, log-home processing or other uses.
Performance measure: current mills still operating and number of new start-up small mills and biomass utilization facilities by state.

Action Item B: Work with Rural Development on a comprehensive approach to increase investments and infrastructure in order to increase biomass utilization in rural communities.
Performance measure: percentage of annual increase in investment by state.

Action Item C: Actively pursue the increased use of portable or on-site options for processing material through the provision of Forest Service grants or other forms of assistance (Rural Development).
Performance measure: number of grants.

Action Item D: Actively pursue the expansion of CHP (combined heat and power) facilities and co-firing (coal and wood) at existing plants, through the provision of grants or other forms of assistance.
Performance measure: number of CHP facilities by State.

Action Item E: Synthesize and conduct research to develop and evaluate various technologies that optimize the use of beetle-killed material, including wood composites, biochemicals, biofuels and biopower. **Performance measure:** Number of research tools developed and applied to management on the ground.

Goal 2: Recovery: Re-establish forests damaged by bark beetles.

Establish desired forest conditions where motility has caused the loss of forest. Healthy forests play a critical role in providing clean water, wildlife habitat, a variety of recreation opportunities and rural jobs. The current infestation has increased fire risk in certain areas and modified wildlife habitats and created the opportunities for establishment of invasive species.

Funding: FY 2011, $5.8 million
Goal Performance measure: FY 2011 17,200 Acres of treatment; FY 2012 81,676 Acres of treatment; FY 2013-2016 661,250 Acres of treatment.

Objective 1: Establish and maintain diverse forest cover.

Action Item A: Strategically place fuel breaks across the landscape to support the use of prescribed fire to reduce fuel loads for reforestation.
Performance measure: Watersheds with hazard mitigated with strategic acres treated.

Action Item B: Seed and plant trees to increase forest diversity and recovery.
Performance measure: acres treated.

Action Item C: Remove invasive plants.
Performance measure: acres successfully treated.

Action Item D: Synthesize and conduct research to determine ecological impacts in terms of changes in function, structure and composition of forested landscapes and the socioeconomic impact to local communities that will lead to improved management decisions for healthy forest reestablishment.
Performance measure: Number of research tools developed and applied to management on the ground.

Goal 3: Resiliency: Prevent or mitigate future bark beetle outbreaks

There is a tremendous opportunity and need to enhance the ecosystem health of western forests at risk from epidemic bark beetle infestations. Bark beetles are native insects not subject to eradication and need to be managed as integral parts of the ecosystem. Resiliency treatments will help prevent and ensure that forests are better able to respond to future bark beetle epidemics, while still maintaining the beetles' role in forest ecosystems. The National Insect and Disease Risk Map (NIDRM) shows where forests are predicted to have greater than 25% mortality between 2006 – 2021, and will be used, along with State Forest Assessments and Strategies, and informed science on treatment impacts to prioritize where treatments will occur to increase forest's resiliency to bark beetle attacks.

> Funding: FY 2011, $8.5 million
> Goal Performance measure: FY 2011 36,800 Acres of treatment; FY 2012 52,110 Acres of treatment; FY 2013-2016 239,327 Acres of treatment.

Objective 1: Increase diversity of age class and tree species in areas that are at the greatest risk.

> **Action Item A:** Apply appropriate silvicultural techniques to create age class diversity, favor species diversity better adapted to drought and create openings in continuous forests to allow natural regeneration to occur.
> **Performance measure:** number of acres treated.

> **Action Item B:** Provide summary and synthesis of relevant research on benefits of increasing vegetation diversity on the population dynamics of various bark beetle species and the silvicultural practices at the landscape level to accomplish these goals.
> **Performance measure:** Number of research tools developed and applied to management on the ground.

Figure 7. Thinning has reduced inter-tree competition around campsites. Region 5, Forest Service

Objective 2: Reduce stand density, where appropriate, to increase resistance to bark-beetle infestation.

> **Action Item A:** Thin overstocked stands to increase spacing between trees, improve tree vigor and retard the spread of bark beetles while being mindful of retention of large diameter trees (Figure 7). In addition, bark beetle suppression work may be completed to protect individual trees and stands.

> **Performance measure:** acres treated.

Action Item B: Apply prescribed fire to certain forests to reduce stand density.
Performance measure: acres treated.

Action Item C: Synthesize and conduct research to better understand the mechanisms by which thinning and other disturbance agents, such as drought, disease, and defoliation, influence tree physiology and thus susceptibility to successful colonization by bark beetles.
Performance measure: Number of research tools developed and applied to management on the ground.

Objective 3: Improve management effectiveness and efficiency through targeted research to fill knowledge gaps on bark beetle dynamics in forest ecosystems.

Action Item A: Synthesize and conduct research on the interaction of bark beetles, fire, drought and climate change; better defining thinning regimes; enhancing predictions of bark beetle population dynamics; and refining how naturally occurring pheromones can be used to manage bark beetle populations. Other topics include modeling fire behavior, recreation uses and experiences in beetle-killed forests, socio-economic impacts on rural communities and wildlife ecology research.
Performance measure: Number of research tools developed and applied to management on the ground.

Action Item B: Synthesize and conduct targeted research on: the basic biology, phenology, and genetic structure of bark beetle populations as a basis for better predicting their response to a changing climate; the interaction of bark beetles, fire, drought and climate change; and the genetic structure of tree populations that are the host for bark beetles to better understand the response of the trees to a changing climate and to better understand the interaction between host and pest in a changing climate to enhance predictions of bark beetle population dynamics. Better understand and predict shifts in range of bark beetles, e.g., northward expansion of southern pine beetle range, eastward expansion of bark beetles from lodgepole to jack pine, and northward expansion of bark beetles from Mexico into SW United States. Develop regional models that will lead to adequate predictions on west-wide climate change impacts on bark beetle dynamics and thus subsequent levels of tree mortality; better define thinning regimes; and refine how naturally occurring pheromones can be used to manage bark beetle populations.
Performance measure: Number of research tools developed and applied to management on the ground.

Objective 4: Create a communication plan to explain the purpose of and the need for bark beetle management.

Action Item A: Develop a communication plan to explain the strategy, including different kinds of products for different audiences and a timeline and a method for delivering these products.
Performance measure: A comprehensive communication plan.

Action Item B: Engage Research and Development and State and Private Forestry Staffs to develop appropriate technology transfer products of the latest bark beetle science and management techniques and share with FS units and partners.
Performance measure: number of published technology transfer products.

Conclusion:

The Forest Service recognizes the bark beetle epidemic has been expanding, and infestations have accelerated in recent years across the west. The situation requires an increased response across the west and will require prioritized placement of treatments, integrating multiple program funds to achieve the maximum amount of priority treatments. Continuing to fund the bark beetle management at the 2010 funding level represents a challenge response in the face of constrained budgets; holding funding constant may represent an increased proportion of the budget, and could result in reductions in other outputs. Outputs that likely will be affected would be road and trail maintenance, recreation facility maintenance, and vegetation treatments outside of bark beetle impact areas. The outcomes of implementing this strategy will be avoidance of people being injured by falling trees, safer communities with reduced fire risk, , less risk to community infrastructure and high-priority watersheds and helping to ensure more resilient forests. If we do not accelerate our management actions to address the bark beetle in the west the public will be at greater risk, and our forests' function will continue to be adversely affected. This is the most cost-effective time to act. It will get more expensive to deal with the safety, recovery, and resiliency issues if we do not act now.

July 11, 2011

Appendices

Appendix 1. Bark Beetle Funding and Projected Accomplishments (in acres) for Fiscal Year 2011, assuming similar agency total appropriation at the final 2010 level.

		FY 2011	
		Outputs (acres)	Dollars ($1000)
Region 1	Safety	15,000	$21,600
	Recovery	2,000	$400
	Resilience	15,500	$2,000
Region 1 Total		**32,500**	**$24,000**
Region 2[12]	Safety	30,700	$30,500
	Recovery	2,400	$700
	Resilience	4,100	$1,800
Region 2 Total		**37,200**	**$33,000**
Region 3	Safety	3,900	$1,500
	Recovery	3,600	$1,100
	Resilience	400	$200
Region 3 Total		**7,900**	**$2,800**
Region 4	Safety	42,700	$6,100
	Recovery	4,200	$2,100
	Resilience	6,400	$800
Region 4 Total		**53,300**	**$9,000**
Region 5	Safety	53,000	$17,100
	Recovery	0	$0
	Resilience	3,700	$1,300
Region 5 Total		**56,700**	**$18,400**
Region 6	Safety	42,500	$8,000
	Recovery	5,000	$1,500
	Resilience	6,700	$2,400
Region 6 Total		**54,200**	**$11,900**
Total	Safety	187,800	$84,800
	Recovery	17,200	$5,800
	Resilience	36,800	$8,500
Grand Total		**241,800**	**$99,100**

---

[12] FY 2010 - Region 2 received an additional $5 million in ARRA Funds and $2 million in carryover in addition to their regular budget.

Appendix 2. Appendix 2 displays the estimated number of acres that regions could potentially accomplish for FY 2012-2016. In some cases, Regions will need to increase capability (personnel, partnerships, and contracting capability) to accomplish this full program level. This represents each Region's estimate of what could be accomplished considering current accomplishments and future planned work, bark beetle risk conditions projected during the time period, and extent of current and past bark beetle epidemic impact. Each Region would need to ramp up from current capability to be able to fully accomplish this full program level presented in Appendix 2. However, actual accomplishments will be a function of actual funding available for this program each fiscal year and this table represents what is realistically possible.

		FY 2012 (acres)	FY 2013 (acres)	FY 2014 (acres)	FY 2015 (acres)	FY 2016 (acres)	Grand Total
Region 1	Safety	52,302	69,825	69,825	55,660	55,660	303,272
	Recovery	49,630	115,230	115,230	124,130	124,130	528.350
	Resilience	10,000	25,300	25,300	38,500	38,500	137,600
Region 1 Total		**111,932**	**210,355**	**210,355**	**218,290**	**218,290**	**969,222**
Region 2	Safety	71,025	81,877	90,271	97,933	107,615	448,721
	Recovery	15,406	27,450	30,288	32,866	36,093	142,103
	Resilience	9,296	976	1,076	1,167	1,283	13,798
Region 2 Total		**95,727**	**110,303**	**121,635**	**131,966**	**144,991**	**604,622**
Region 3	Safety	6,050	8,100	12,250	11,500	8,500	46,400
	Recovery	1,700	0	0	0	0	1,700
	Resilience	6,300	9,400	7,250	8,000	5,500	36,450
Region 3 Total		**14,050**	**17,500**	**19,500**	**19,500**	**14,000**	**84,550**
Region 4	Safety	46,616	58,271	69,925	87,406	87,406	349,624
	Recovery	3,740	4,049	4,358	2,813	2,813	17,773
	Resilience	6,164	7,091	8,018	3,383	3,383	28,039
Region 4 Total		**56,520**	**69,411**	**82,301**	**93,602**	**93,602**	**395,436**
Region 5	Safety	14,800	19,300	19,300	19,300	19,300	92,000
	Recovery	0	0	0	0	0	0
	Resilience	13,700	10,000	10,000	10,000	10,000	53,700
Region 5 Total		**28,500**	**29,300**	**29,300**	**29,300**	**29,300**	**145,700**
Region 6	Safety	49,233	33,000	32925	77,000	78,050	270,208
	Recovery	11,200	11,600	11,000	9,600	9,600	53,000
	Resilience	6,650	3,600	4,000	4,000	3,600	21,850
Region 6 Total		**67,083**	**48,200**	**47,925**	**90,600**	**91250**	**345,058**
Total	Safety	240,026	270,373	294,4 96	348,799	356,531	1,510,225
	Recovery	81,676	158,329	160,876	169,409	172,636	742,926
	Resilience	52,110	56,367	55,644	65,050	62,266	291,437
Grand Total		**373,812**	**485,069**	**511,016**	**583,258**	**591,433**	**2,544,588**

Appendix 3. Projected Capability (in acres) from Fiscal Years 2012 – 2016. Appendix 3 displays the projected accomplishments as a straight line projection of the FY-2011 funded program of work compared to the potential projected accomplishment with an unconstrained budget.

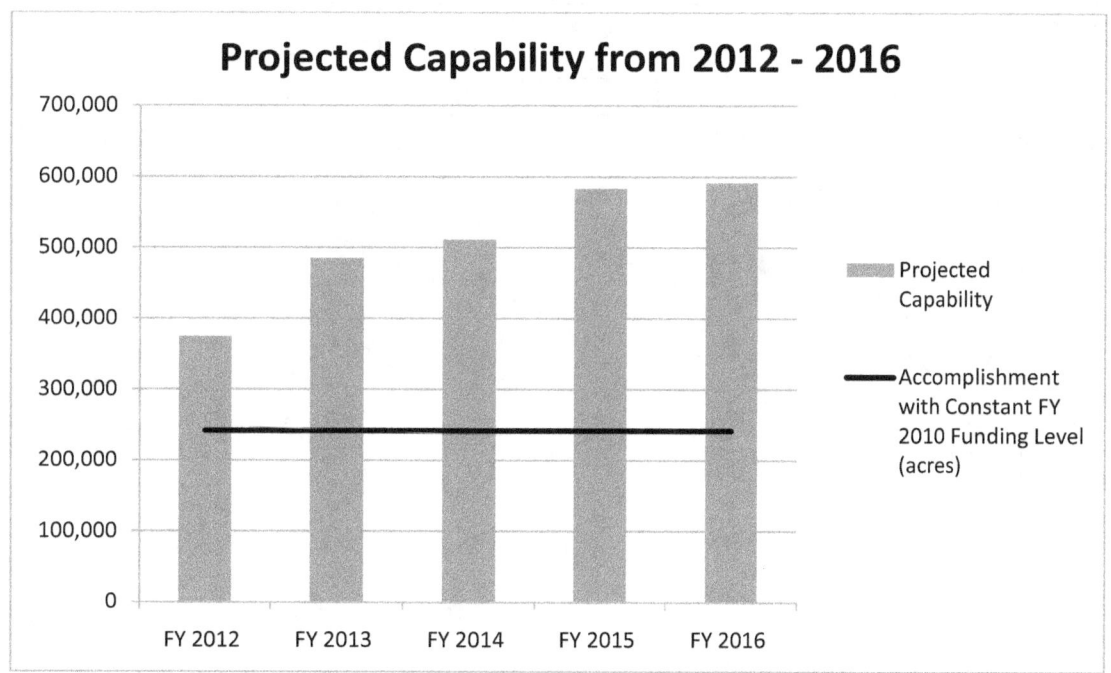

The FY 2011-2016 planned accomplishment is based on maintaining the FY 2010 funding level and agency total appropriations similar to FY 2010. Actual accomplishment will depend on the actual final appropriation the agency receives in the out years.

July 11, 2011

Appendix 4. Projected Research Funding for Fiscal Year 2011 – 2016 ($1000)

		2011	2012	2013	2014	2015	2016	Total
R & D	Safety	$750	$750	$750	$750	$750	$750	$4,500
	Recovery	$200	$200	$200	$200	$200	$200	$1,200
	Resilience	$1,500	$1,500	$1,500	$1,500	$1,500	$1,500	$9,000
R & D Total		**$2,450**	**$2,450**	**$2,450**	**$2,450**	**$2,450**	**$2,450**	**$14,700**

Appendix 4 displays the Research and Development funding necessary to support the three goals of Safety, Recovery and Resiliency.

SUCCESS STORIES

Thinning Overstocked Stands within the Lake Davis Recreation Area

Figure 1. Dense eastside pine stands at Lake Davis.

Western Bark Beetle Initiative (WBBI) funds were utilized to thin 306 acres of densely stocked ponderosa and Jeffrey pine forest within the Lake Davis Recreation Area, Beckwourth Ranger District, Plumas National Forest. The Lake Davis Thinning Project was a collaborative effort between the Beckwourth Ranger District and Forest Health Protection to increase resistance of ponderosa and Jeffrey pines to successful bark beetle attacks. The WBBI funding enabled the District to increase the resiliency of eastside pine forests, consistent with ecological restoration goals, reduce hazardous fuels and improve bald eagle nesting habitat within this high-use recreation area.

Forested areas around Lake Davis contained an overstory of scattered, large diameter ponderosa and Jeffrey pine that were experiencing excessive competition from sapling and pole-sized pines and white firs (Figure 1). Most stands were stocked at levels considered highly susceptible to bark beetle caused tree mortality (stand density index or SDI ranged from 250 to 580 and basal area ranged from 120 to 400 ft^2/acre). These conditions were allowing Jeffrey, western and mountain pine beetles to successfully attack and kill many large diameter pines around the lake as well as increasing the risk of large scale tree mortality within campgrounds and bald eagle habitat.

The treatments consisted of thinning stands to a range of sustainable stocking levels (SDI 200 - 270 or 80 – 140 ft^2/acre) (Figure 2), generally retaining higher stand densities around picnic areas and special wildlife habitat zones to provide greater canopy cover. Stands are now more open and growing conditions are greatly enhanced due to less inter-tree competition (Figure 3). This project provided 3,230 CCF of saw logs to a local mill and 3,416 CCF of chips for local biomass energy production (a total of ~19,000 tons of wood fiber removed).

Figure 2. Tree removal within Grizzly Campground

Figure 3. Thinning treatments have reduced inter-tree competition around campsites.

This project has resulted in improved forest health and resiliency by reducing stocking levels in stands that were previously susceptible to significant negative impacts from bark beetles. Post-treatment stand densities will now sustain and enhance individual tree health and vigor well into the future, and, combined with the reduction in ladder fuels, will significantly reduce the intensity of any wildfire.

This high visibility project will also provide the District with a great example of active forest management. Approximately 200,000 annual visitors will be able to read project interpretation signs displayed at campground entrances and selected access roads that explain bark beetle biology, why trees were removed and the long-term benefits of forest thinning.

For more information, contact Danny Cluck at (530) 252-6431

SUCCESS STORIES

Forest Thinning Protects Communities and Critical Wildlife Habitat

Forest Health Protection prevention funds were utilized to thin approximately 592 acres of densely stocked ponderosa and Jeffrey pine forest within the Urban Wildland Interface Zone next to Eagle Lake and the community of Spalding, Eagle Lake Ranger District, Lassen National Forest. The Spalding Wildland Urban Interface Project (Figure 1) was part of a collaborative effort between the Spalding community, Lassen National Forest and Forest Health Protection to reduce hazardous fuel loads surrounding this residential and recreation area and to improve and enhance the existing bald eagle nesting habitat found along the shore of Eagle Lake by accelerating the development of large trees and improving conifer resistance to bark beetle attack.

Stands in the Spalding area contained an overstory of scattered, large diameter ponderosa and Jeffrey pine with an overstocked understory of sapling and pole-sized pines. Stand densities ranged from 89 to 176 square feet/acre. Jeffrey and western pine beetle activity was reducing the number of large diameter trees which are essential for bald eagle nesting and roosting habitat. Additionally, ladder fuels created by the dense thickets of understory trees and an accumulation of course woody debris, fine surface litter and duff had put the entire area at risk to a stand replacing wildfire. Historically, these stands would have experienced frequent low intensity wildfires that would have kept understory trees and fuels at a minimum. Natural fire has now been excluded from the project area for well over ninety years, resulting in as many as 12 missed fire cycles.

Figure 1. Spalding Wildland Urban Interface project.

The Forest Health Protection funded project consisted of thinning overstocked stands on public lands surrounding hundreds of private residences and four active bald eagle nests. These treatments took a "thin from below" approach to ensure that the largest trees would remain post-treatment. Following the treatment in 2005/2006, at a cost of $190/acre, the stands contained an average of 60 - 90 square feet of basal area, post-treatment ladder fuels were minimal and understory fuels averaged 2-3 tons per acre (Figures 2 & 3). It is estimated that these treatments have left approximately 40 to 100 trees per acre at a variable spacing that focused on giving individual large diameter trees additional growing space and retaining existing clumps of large trees regardless of spacing. These stocking densities will likely sustain stands in a healthy condition for a period of at least twenty years.

This project has resulted in improved forest health and resiliency by reducing stocking levels in stands that were susceptible to significant impacts from bark beetles and stand replacing wildfire. Post-treatment stand densities will now sustain and enhance individual tree health and vigor well into the future, and, combined with the reduction in surface and ladder fuels, will significantly reduce wildfire intensity. Residual stand conditions will now allow the use of prescribed fire to maintain minimal fuel loads while providing this landscape the natural disturbance needed to function as a fire-dependant ecosystem.

Figure 2. Before treatment, dense pine stands were highly susceptible to bark beetle attacks and catastrophic wildfire.

Figure 3. After treatment, thinned stands are much more resilient to the affects of bark beetles and wildfire.

For more information, contact Danny Cluck at (530) 252-6431   *June 30, 2007*

SUCCESS STORIES

Forest Thinning Protects Communities and Critical Wildlife Habitat

Forest Health Protection prevention funds were utilized to thin approximately 592 acres of densely stocked ponderosa and Jeffrey pine forest within the Urban Wildland Interface Zone next to Eagle Lake and the community of Spalding, Eagle Lake Ranger District, Lassen National Forest. The Spalding Wildland Urban Interface Project (Figure 1) was part of a collaborative effort between the Spalding community, Lassen National Forest and Forest Health Protection to reduce hazardous fuel loads surrounding this residential and recreation area and to improve and enhance the existing bald eagle nesting habitat found along the shore of Eagle Lake by accelerating the development of large trees and improving conifer resistance to bark beetle attack.

Stands in the Spalding area contained an overstory of scattered, large diameter ponderosa and Jeffrey pine with an overstocked understory of sapling and pole-sized pines. Stand densities ranged from 89 to 176 square feet/acre. Jeffrey and western pine beetle activity was reducing the number of large diameter trees which are essential for bald eagle nesting and roosting habitat. Additionally, ladder fuels created by the dense thickets of understory trees and an accumulation of course woody debris, fine surface litter and duff had put the entire area at risk to a stand replacing wildfire. Historically, these stands would have experienced frequent low intensity wildfires that would have kept understory trees and fuels at a minimum. Natural fire has now been excluded from the project area for well over ninety years, resulting in as many as 12 missed fire cycles.

Figure 1. Spalding Wildland Urban Interface project.

The Forest Health Protection funded project consisted of thinning overstocked stands on public lands surrounding hundreds of private residences and four active bald eagle nests. These treatments took a "thin from below" approach to ensure that the largest trees would remain post-treatment. Following the treatment in 2005/2006, at a cost of $190/acre, the stands contained an average of 60 - 90 square feet of basal area, post-treatment ladder fuels were minimal and understory fuels averaged 2-3 tons per acre (Figures 2 & 3). It is estimated that these treatments have left approximately 40 to 100 trees per acre at a variable spacing that focused on giving individual large diameter trees additional growing space and retaining existing clumps of large trees regardless of spacing. These stocking densities will likely sustain stands in a healthy condition for a period of at least twenty years.

This project has resulted in improved forest health and resiliency by reducing stocking levels in stands that were susceptible to significant impacts from bark beetles and stand replacing wildfire. Post-treatment stand densities will now sustain and enhance individual tree health and vigor well into the future, and, combined with the reduction in surface and ladder fuels, will significantly reduce wildfire intensity. Residual stand conditions will now allow the use of prescribed fire to maintain minimal fuel loads while providing this landscape the natural disturbance needed to function as a fire-dependant ecosystem.

Figure 2. Before treatment, dense pine stands were highly susceptible to bark beetle attacks and catastrophic wildfire.

Figure 3. After treatment, thinned stands are much more resilient to the affects of bark beetles and wildfire.

Protecting an Investment:
Forest thinning and fuel reduction enables trees to survive wildfire.

In 2009, the Station Fire impacted 160,577 acres, primarily on the Angeles National Forest (Figure 1). The wildfire encompassed much of the Los Angeles Ranger District and numerous Western Bark Beetle Initiative (WBBI) funded projects.

For several years prior to the wildfire, Forest Health Protection (FHP) was collaborating with the Ranger District to protect forests from bark beetles and wildfire in the Charlton-Chilao Picnic Area and Campground. In 2007, when bark beetles were threatening ponderosa pine within the picnic area, high-value trees were treated across 175 acres with FHP funding ($70,000). These insecticide treatments prevented successful beetle attacks on the pines which are critical ecosystem components and also enhance recreational and scenic values. In addition, preventive tree thinning and fuel reduction work have been on-going in Charlton-Chilao to improve residual tree health and vigor.

FHP dollars ($400,000) combined with fuels funding resulted in thinning 700 acres in and surrounding this high-use area. These treatments reduced the susceptibility of pines to successful bark beetle attacks and reduced fuel loading.

The Station wildfire severely impacted forest stands in the Charlton-Chilao picnic area and campground (Figure 2). However, tree thinning and fuel reduction treatments protected much of the recreation area (Figure 3). Trees in the treated areas were minimally impacted and survived the wildfire. Large-scale, multi-year preventive tree thinning and fuel reduction projects resulted in protecting the trees in this valuable, high-use destination.

Figure 1. Station Fire caused tree mortality and injury on the Angeles National Forest

Figure 2. Untreated forest stands in the Charlton-Chilao picnic area were devastated by wildfire.

Figure 3. Thinned stands in the picnic area that were protected from the wildfire.

For more information, contact Tom Coleman, Entomologist, at (909)382-2871 or twcoleman@fs.fed.us
May 30, 2010.